Kitchen Science

# Science Experiments
## THAT
# SURPRISE
## AND
# DELIGHT

### Fun Projects for Curious Kids

by Sheri Bell-Rehwoldt

CAPSTONE PRESS
a capstone imprint

Edge Books are published by Capstone Press,
151 Good Counsel Drive, P.O. Box 669, Mankato, Minnesota 56002.
www.capstonepub.com

*Library of Congress Cataloging-in-Publication Data*
Bell-Rehwoldt, Sheri.
  Science experiments that surprise and delight : fun projects for curious
kids / by Sheri Bell-Rehwoldt.
    p. cm.—(Edge books. Kitchen science)
  Summary: "Provides step-by-step instructions for science projects using
household materials and explains the science behind the experiments"—Provided
by publisher.
  Includes bibliographical references and index.
  ISBN 978-1-4296-5428-9 (library binding)
  ISBN 978-1-4296-6253-6 (paperback)
  1. Science—Experiments—Juvenile literature.  I. Title. II. Series.

  Q182.3.B435 2011
  507.8—dc22
                                                    2010025205

**Editorial Credits**
Lori Shores, editor; Veronica Correia, designer; Eric Manske, production specialist;
   Sarah Schuette, photo stylist; Marcy Morin, studio scheduler; Wanda Winch,
   media researcher

**Photo Credits**
All photos by Capstone Studio/Karon Dubke

Printed in the United States of America in Stevens Point, Wisconsion.
092010       005934WZS11

# TABLE OF Contents

# Introduction

Some science experiments require a fancy laboratory with special equipment. But other experiments can be done just about anywhere, like in your own kitchen. And many great projects can even be done with things you have around your house.

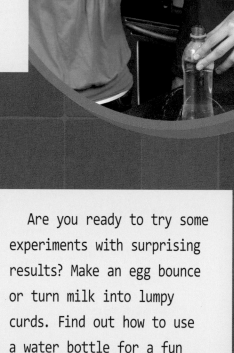

Are you ready to try some experiments with surprising results? Make an egg bounce or turn milk into lumpy curds. Find out how to use a water bottle for a fun prank. Use a lemon to learn how batteries work.

Some of these projects may require the help of an adult. But most of them can be done on your own. Just be sure to follow any safety tips. And remember, science is awesome, but it's rarely without a mess. Some post-project clean-up may be needed. After all, you don't want your parents to shut down your lab. Get ready to be surprised and delighted by science in the kitchen!

# Dancing Raisins

Maybe you've heard of the California raisins. Those raisins loved to show off their dance moves, even if they were just cartoon characters. But all raisins will dance if you give them a chance. Drop them in a glass of fizzy soda to see the show.

## What you need:

- drinking glass
- clear soda
- five raisins

Do other items rise and sink in soda? Try grapes or uncooked macaroni and see what happens.

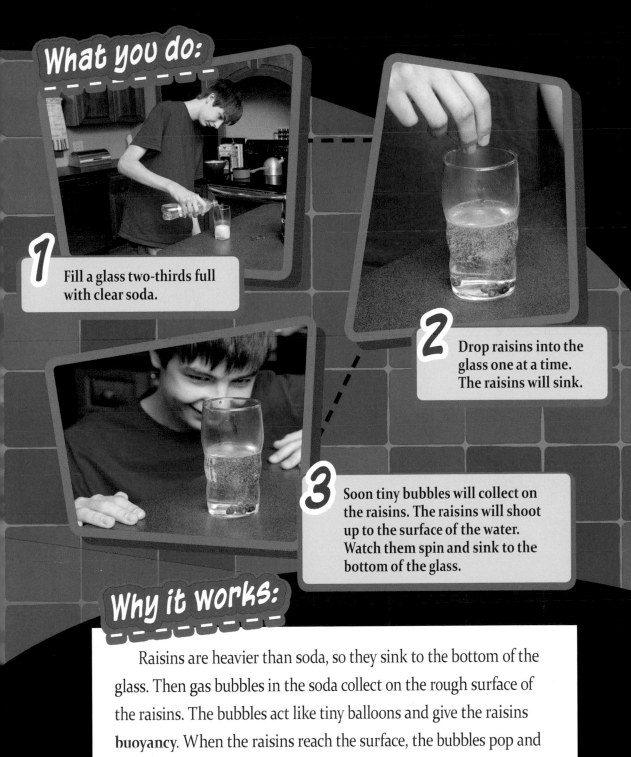

## What you do:

**1** Fill a glass two-thirds full with clear soda.

**2** Drop raisins into the glass one at a time. The raisins will sink.

**3** Soon tiny bubbles will collect on the raisins. The raisins will shoot up to the surface of the water. Watch them spin and sink to the bottom of the glass.

## Why it works:

Raisins are heavier than soda, so they sink to the bottom of the glass. Then gas bubbles in the soda collect on the rough surface of the raisins. The bubbles act like tiny balloons and give the raisins **buoyancy**. When the raisins reach the surface, the bubbles pop and the gas escapes into the air. Then the raisins sink back to the bottom.

**buoyancy**—the ability to rise or float in liquid

# Too Many Straws

A straw makes it easy to drink a glass of water. Using two straws should make it even easier and faster, right? Try this experiment yourself to see if two straws are better than one.

## What you need:

- drinking glass
- water
- two straws

## What you do:

**1** Fill a glass with water about three-fourths full.

**2** Place one straw inside the glass. Hold the other straw outside the glass.

**3** Place both straws in your mouth and try to take a drink. No matter how hard you try, you won't be able to suck up any water!

This is a fun trick to play on a friend. Tell her that you can finish a drink faster with one straw than she can with two straws. Then watch as she tries to take a drink.

## Why it works:

When you drink from a straw, you first suck the air out of the straw, leaving no **air pressure** there to hold the liquid down. But air pressure is still pushing down on the rest of the liquid in the glass. That air pressure causes the liquid to push up through the straw. But when you used two straws, the straw outside the glass pulled air into your mouth. That kept the air pressure in the first straw the same. The air pressure in your mouth and straw kept the liquid from coming up through the straw.

air pressure—the weight of air

# Salt and Pepper Separator

Sure, you could try to separate salt and pepper by hand. Or you could just blow up a balloon and do it the easy way.

## What you need:

- 1 teaspoon (5 mL) salt
- 1 teaspoon (5 mL) pepper
- small plate
- balloon
- measuring spoon

## What you do:

1. Sprinkle the salt and pepper onto a small plate.

Need another way to separate salt and pepper? Pour the salt and pepper into a glass of water. The salt will dissolve in the water, but the pepper will float.

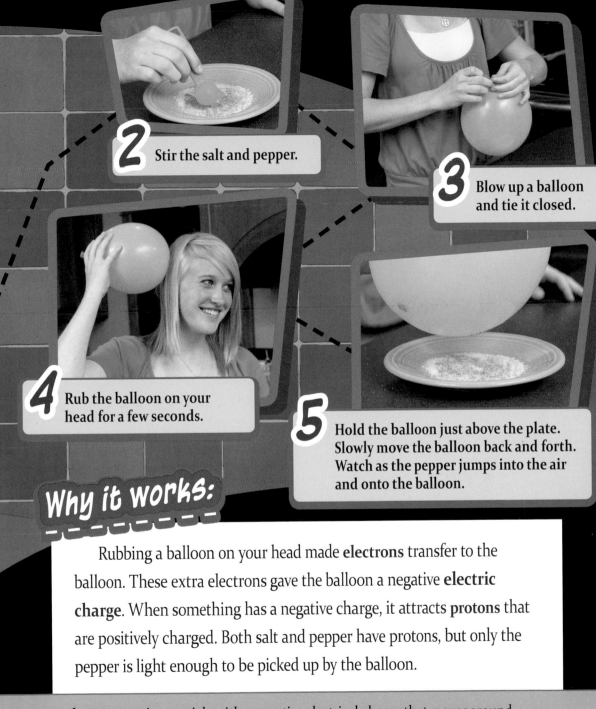

**2** Stir the salt and pepper.

**3** Blow up a balloon and tie it closed.

**4** Rub the balloon on your head for a few seconds.

**5** Hold the balloon just above the plate. Slowly move the balloon back and forth. Watch as the pepper jumps into the air and onto the balloon.

## Why it works:

Rubbing a balloon on your head made **electrons** transfer to the balloon. These extra electrons gave the balloon a negative **electric charge**. When something has a negative charge, it attracts **protons** that are positively charged. Both salt and pepper have protons, but only the pepper is light enough to be picked up by the balloon.

**electron**—a tiny particle with a negative electrical charge that moves around the nucleus of an atom

**electric charge**—the amount of electricity in an object

**proton**—a tiny particle with a positive electrical charge that moves around the nucleus of an atom

# Apple Jab

Do you have a friend who is always bragging about his muscles? He should have no problem poking a straw through an apple, right? When he can't do it, show him how it's done. It's not muscle power he'll need. It's science power!

## What you need:

- plastic drinking straw
- apple

## What you do:

**1** Hand your friend a straw and an apple. Have him try to poke the straw into an apple. He won't be able to do it.

**2** Wrap one hand around the apple. Hold the straw in your other hand. Cover the top of the straw with your thumb.

**3** Jab the open end of the straw through the side of the apple. The straw should easily enter the apple without bending.

You can also try this project with a raw potato.

## Why it works:

A straw might look empty to you, but it is really filled with air. When you cover one end of a straw with your thumb, air can't escape from that end. When the straw hits the apple, both ends of the straw become sealed. The trapped air pushes against the sides of the straw from the inside. This pressure makes the straw strong enough to pierce through the apple.

# Bottle Surprise

Did you know that you could fill a bottle with water, punch holes in it, and not get wet? It's true! The water stays put until air pressure starts pushing on it.

## What you need:

- plastic drink bottle
- water
- pushpin

This experiment makes the perfect prank. Wait until you're outside, and offer your friend a drink. When your friend twists off the cap, she will be in for a wet surprise!

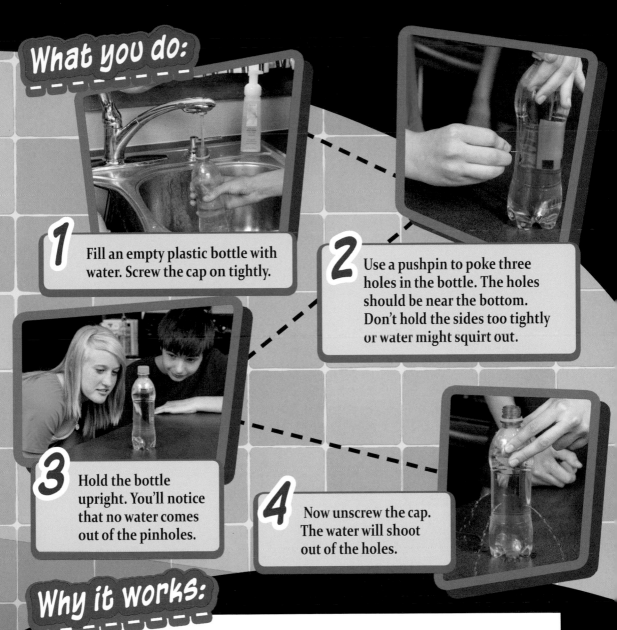

**1** Fill an empty plastic bottle with water. Screw the cap on tightly.

**2** Use a pushpin to poke three holes in the bottle. The holes should be near the bottom. Don't hold the sides too tightly or water might squirt out.

**3** Hold the bottle upright. You'll notice that no water comes out of the pinholes.

**4** Now unscrew the cap. The water will shoot out of the holes.

# Why it works:

Air in the bottle escaped as you filled the bottle with water. With the cap on, no more air could get in. But air is all around the bottle, pushing down on the cap and against the sides. The small holes in the bottle weren't big enough for more air to sneak in and increase the air pressure on the water. But when you opened the cap, more air got in and pressed down on the water, sending it shooting from the holes.

# LiQUiD or SOLiD?

It's usually easy to tell whether something is a liquid or a solid. Your kitchen table is a solid. Lemonade is a liquid. But when you combine cornstarch and water, you end up with a mystery!

## What you need:

- 2 cups (480 mL) cornstarch
- mixing bowl
- 1 cup (240 mL) water
- a few drops of food coloring
- spoon

## What you do:

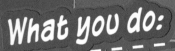

 Pour the cornstarch into a bowl.

 Measure the water and add a few drops of food coloring. Stir to mix.

**3** Slowly add the water and food coloring to the cornstarch.

**4** Mix the ingredients together. The mixture should be thick and difficult to stir. If it's too thick to stir, add a little more water to the mixture.

**5** Gently press your fist into the mixture. It should easily sink in. Now try punching it hard. Your fist can't sink in!

**6** Put your hand in the mixture again. Try pulling it out quickly. Then try again, but this time raise your hand slowly.

## Why it works:

Water and cornstarch don't mix completely. Cornstarch **molecules** tangle up with each other, and water molecules flow around them. When you move your hand slowly through the mixture, those tangled molecules have time to move out of the way. But when you move quickly, the molecules can't move, and the water can't flow around your hand.

molecule—the atoms making up the smallest unit of a substance

# Waterproof Paper

When you put a paper towel under water, you expect it to get soaked. Keep the paper towel dry by putting science to work. Grab an audience, because this project is a showstopper!

## What you need:

- large mixing bowl
- water
- paper towel
- small drinking glass

## What you do:

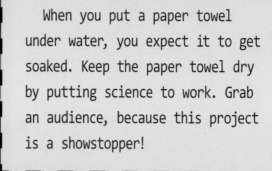

**1** Fill the mixing bowl three-fourths full of water.

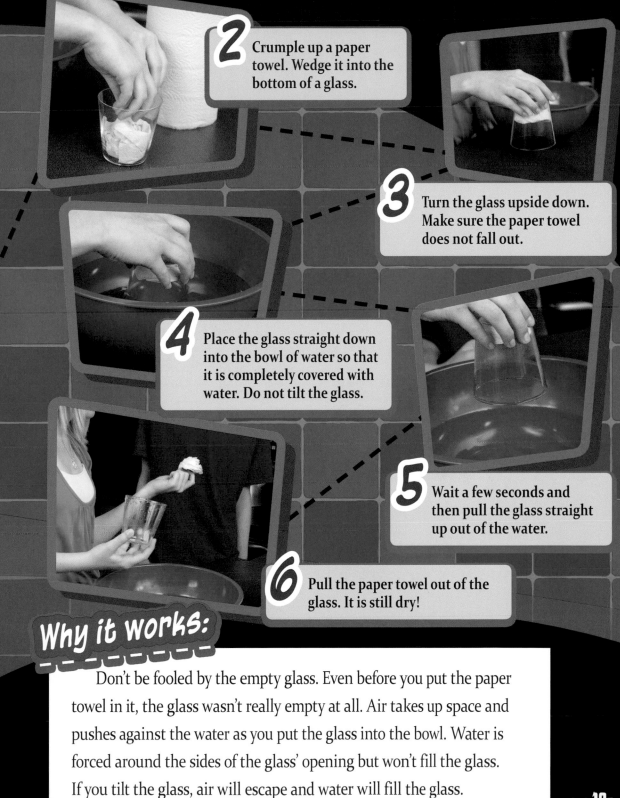

**2** Crumple up a paper towel. Wedge it into the bottom of a glass.

**3** Turn the glass upside down. Make sure the paper towel does not fall out.

**4** Place the glass straight down into the bowl of water so that it is completely covered with water. Do not tilt the glass.

**5** Wait a few seconds and then pull the glass straight up out of the water.

**6** Pull the paper towel out of the glass. It is still dry!

## Why it works:

Don't be fooled by the empty glass. Even before you put the paper towel in it, the glass wasn't really empty at all. Air takes up space and pushes against the water as you put the glass into the bowl. Water is forced around the sides of the glass' opening but won't fill the glass. If you tilt the glass, air will escape and water will fill the glass.

# Electric Lemon

You know that lemons have plenty of pucker power. But did you know that they also have battery power? Inside that bumpy, yellow skin is a natural battery.

## What you do:

## What you need:

- paper clip
- lemon
- 3-inch (8-cm) piece of copper wire

**1** Unbend the paper clip.

**2** Roll the lemon on a table. Push down with your palm until you feel the juice flowing under the peel.

**3** Pierce the lemon with the paper clip.

**4** Poke the copper wire into the lemon near the paper clip.

**5** Touch the ends of the paper clip and copper wire to the tip of your tongue. You should feel a slight tingle.

## Why it works:

Batteries are made with two different metals and an **acid**. One of the metals contains a positive electric charge. The other metal contains a negative electric charge. For this battery, the paper clip and copper wire provide the positive and negative charges. The lemon creates the acid. When your tongue is on the wires, it completes a **circuit**. Take your tongue away, and you break the circuit.

acid—a substance with a sour taste that reacts easily with other substances
circuit—a path for electricity to flow through

# Bouncing Egg

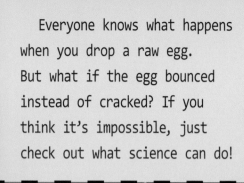

Everyone knows what happens when you drop a raw egg. But what if the egg bounced instead of cracked? If you think it's impossible, just check out what science can do!

## What you need:

- egg
- glass jar with lid
- vinegar

You can try a similar experiment with a chicken leg bone. Cover the bone in vinegar and store it in a covered jar for three days. The bone will become rubbery.

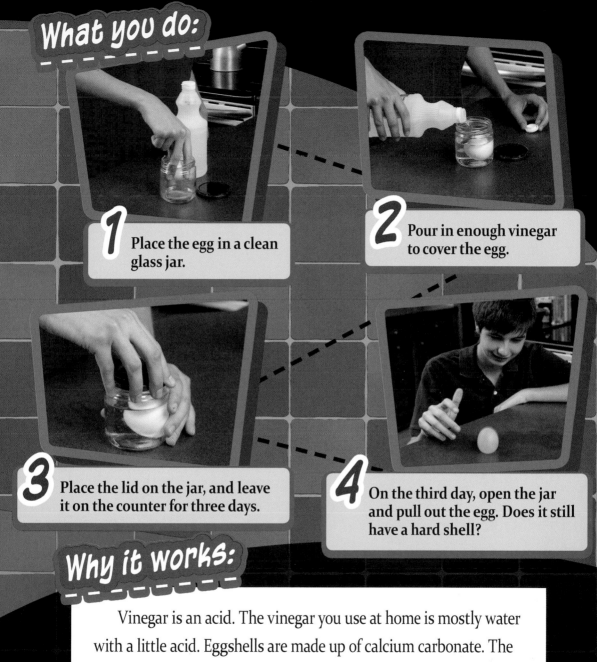

**1** Place the egg in a clean glass jar.

**2** Pour in enough vinegar to cover the egg.

**3** Place the lid on the jar, and leave it on the counter for three days.

**4** On the third day, open the jar and pull out the egg. Does it still have a hard shell?

## Why it works:

Vinegar is an acid. The vinegar you use at home is mostly water with a little acid. Eggshells are made up of calcium carbonate. The vinegar causes the shell to break down into carbon dioxide **gas** and lime. The lime mixes with the water in the jar, and the carbon dioxide escapes into the air. The shell breaks down completely, and you're left with only the soft tissue that lines the inside.

**gas**—a substance that spreads to fill any space that holds it

# Lumpy Milk

If you have ever eaten cottage cheese, you've had curds and whey. The curds are the lumpy parts, and the whey is the liquid. Mix milk and vinegar to make your own lumpy glue. Then try the tip and add baking soda to make it even stickier.

## What you need:

- 1 cup (240 mL) whole milk
- small saucepan
- 1 teaspoon (5 mL) white vinegar
- wooden spoon
- strainer
- spoon
- paper towel

## What you do:

**1** Pour the milk into a saucepan.

**2** Ask an adult to heat the milk on the stove at medium heat for 4 to 5 minutes.

**3** Add vinegar to the pan and stir. The milk will begin to boil and form solid lumps.

**4** When you have several lumps, remove the pan from the stove. Have an adult strain the liquid into a bowl.

**5** Pat the lumps in the strainer with the spoon to remove as much liquid as possible.

**6** Remove the ball from the strainer. Let it cool on a paper towel before using as glue.

Add 1 teaspoon (5 mL) each of water and baking soda to the lumpy milk. Let it sit overnight, and it will be even stickier.

## Why it works:

Milk is both a liquid and solid. It contains a tasteless, odorless protein called casein. When the casein combines with the acid in the vinegar, the solids turn into curds. The liquid part of the milk is the whey. When the whey is combined with the vinegar, a sticky substance is formed.

# Layer Magic

The best part of a rain shower is the rainbow that gets left behind. You can make your own indoor rainbow anytime by combining some common household liquids.

## What you need:

- 1/4 cup (60 mL) light corn syrup
- tall glass jar or pitcher with smooth, straight sides
- 1/4 cup (60 mL) blue dish soap
- spoon
- green food coloring
- 1/4 cup (60 mL) water
- 1/4 cup (60 mL) vegetable oil
- red food coloring
- 1/4 cup (60 mL) rubbing alcohol

# What you do:

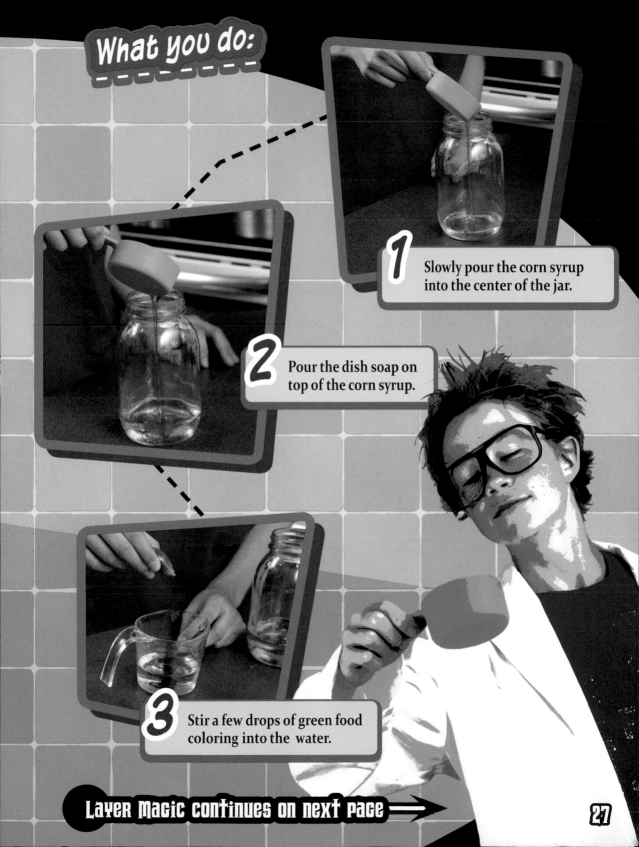

**1** Slowly pour the corn syrup into the center of the jar.

**2** Pour the dish soap on top of the corn syrup.

**3** Stir a few drops of green food coloring into the water.

Layer Magic continues on next page ➡

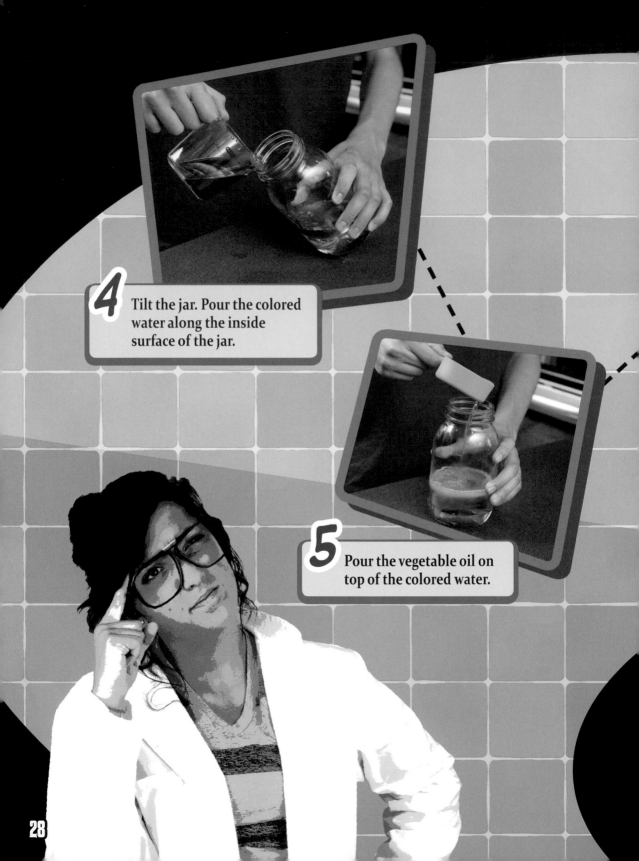

**4** Tilt the jar. Pour the colored water along the inside surface of the jar.

**5** Pour the vegetable oil on top of the colored water.

**6** Stir a few drops of red food coloring into the rubbing alcohol.

Unless you are instructed to pour a liquid along the inside of the jar, try not to let the liquids touch the sides as you pour them.

**7** Tilt the jar. Pour the rubbing alcohol along the inside surface of the jar. Hold the jar up to the light and admire the layered rainbow.

## Why it works:

Each liquid has a different weight. Lighter liquids have a lower **density**. This means they will float on top of liquids that weigh more. Each liquid poured into the jar weighs less than the liquid poured before it. Dish soap weighs less than corn syrup. Water weighs less than dish soap. Rather than mix together, the liquids float on top of one another to create a colorful rainbow.

**density**—how heavy or light something is for its size

# GLOSSARY

**acid** (AS-id)—a substance with a sour taste that reacts easily with other substances

**air pressure** (AIR PRESH-ur)—the weight of air; pressure is the force produced by pressing on something

**buoyancy** (BOI-en-see)—the ability to rise or float in liquid

**circuit** (SUHR-kuht)—a path for electricity to flow through

**density** (DEN-si-tee)—how heavy or light something is for its size

**electric charge** (i-LEK-trik CHARJ)—the amount of electricity that is in an object; an object can have a negative or positive charge

**electron** (i-LEK-tron)—a tiny particle that moves around the nucleus of an atom; electrons carry a negative electrical charge

**gas** (GASS)—a substance that spreads to fill any space that holds it

**molecule** (MOL-uh-kyool)—the atoms that make up the smallest unit of a substance

**proton** (PROH-ton)—one of the very small parts in the nucleus of an atom; a proton carries a positive electrical charge

# Read More

**Bardhan-Quallen, Sudipta.** *Kitchen Science Experiments: How Does Your Mold Garden Grow?* Mad Science. New York: Sterling, 2010.

**Mills, J. Elizabeth.** *The Everything Kids' Easy Science Experiments Book: Explore the World of Science Through Quick and Fun Experiments!* Everything Kids. Avon, Mass.: Adams Media, 2010.

**Wheeler-Toppen, Jodi.** *Science Experiments that Explode and Implode.* Kitchen Science. Mankato, Minn.: Capstone Press, 2011.

# Internet Sites

FactHound offers a safe, fun way to find Internet sites related to this book. All of the sites on FactHound have been researched by our staff.

Here's all you do:

Visit *www.facthound.com*

Type in this code: **9781429654289**

Check out projects, games and lots more at
**www.capstonekids.com**

# Index